# QUEEN ESTHER

Under the direction of Romain Lizé, CEO, Magnificat
Editor, Magnificat: Isabelle Galmiche
Editor, Ignatius: Vivian Dudro
Proofreader: Kathleen Hollenbeck
Assistant to the Editor: Pascale van de Walle
Layout Designer: Magali Meunier
Production: Thierry Dubus, Sabine Marioni

First published by Harper & Row, New York, NY
© 1986 by Tomie dePaola

ISBN Ignatius Press 978-1-62164-370-8 • ISBN Magnificat 978-1-949239-26-3

# TOMIE DE PAOLA
# QUEEN ESTHER

MAGNIFICAT · Ignatius

This is the story of a brave
and beautiful woman named Esther.
Esther lived in Persia
with her older cousin, Mordecai.
Mordecai raised Esther as his own daughter
after her parents died.
Esther and Mordecai were Jews.

The king of Persia was named Ahasuerus. He was looking for a woman to be his new queen and wife, and he asked that beautiful young women be brought before him. Esther was among these young women.

King Ahasuerus admired Esther more than all the others.
So he chose Esther to be his queen.

King Ahasuerus did not know Esther was Jewish. The Jewish people followed the laws God gave to Moses. Some of these laws were different from the laws and customs of Persia. Because of this difference, some people in Persia hated the Jews. Esther's cousin Mordecai warned Esther not to tell anyone that she was Jewish, not even the king.

After a time, King Ahasuerus made Mordecai an official in the palace. The king did not know that Queen Esther and Mordecai were related.
And the king still did not know that Esther was Jewish.

One day, in the palace, Mordecai heard some men planning to kill the king. Mordecai told Esther, and she warned the king. King Ahasuerus was grateful to Queen Esther, and he loved her very much.

Several years passed, and then King Ahasuerus made an evil and jealous man named Haman his chief official.

The king commanded all the other officials to bow down before Haman.
Mordecai would not bow!

"I am a Jew," he explained, "and will not bow to Haman."

Haman became so angry at Mordecai that he wanted to kill him. And because Mordecai was a Jew and obeyed the Jewish law, Haman wanted to kill every Jew in the whole kingdom. First Haman cast lots, like rolling dice, to find out the right day and month to carry out his plan. (These lots were called *purim*.)

Next, Haman went to King Ahasuerus. "There is a certain race of people in Persia who are different," Haman said. "They do not follow the customs and laws of the land." Haman asked the king to have these people, the Jews, put to death. King Ahasuerus listened, and then he ordered that the Jews be killed.

When the Jews heard the king's order, they were frightened. They cried and wailed. Mordecai ripped his clothes, put on sackcloth, and covered his head with ashes.

**W**ailing loudly and bitterly,
he walked through the city
to the palace. But he did not go in.

Queen Esther became very upset
when she heard what Mordecai was doing.
She sent one of her servants to Mordecai
to find out what had happened.
Mordecai sent a message back to Esther.
He told her about the king's order.
He begged her to speak to King Ahasuerus
and to save her people.

"I cannot go to see the king unless he sends for me,"
Queen Esther said. "Anyone who goes to the king
without being called will be put to death."
But Mordecai warned Esther, saying,
"You must not keep quiet at a time like this.
Perhaps it was for this reason you were made queen."

Then Esther sent a message to all the Jews.
She asked them to pray and fast for three days.
She and her servants would do the same.
"Then I will go to King Ahasuerus," she said.
"If I must die to do it, I will die."

After three days of prayer and fasting, Esther put on her royal robes and went to King Ahasuerus. When she stood before him, the king remembered how much he loved her. He raised his royal scepter, and Esther came near and touched it.

"What do you want, Queen Esther?" Ahasuerus asked. "Tell me, and you shall have it."

"If it please Your Majesty," said Esther, "I would like you and Haman to be my guests tonight at a banquet I am preparing for you."

For two days in a row, Esther had banquets
for Ahasuerus and Haman. At each one the king
asked her, "What do you want, Queen Esther?
Tell me, and you shall have it, even up to half my kingdom."

At last Esther said, "If it please Your Majesty, my wish is that I may live, and that my people may live. We are about to be killed."

"Who dares to do such a thing?" asked Ahasuerus.

Esther replied, "Our enemy is this cruel man, Haman."

The king leaped up in fury, and Haman looked at the king and queen in terror. Then one of the servants told the king that Haman had built a gallows for Mordecai, the man who had saved the king's life. "Hang Haman himself on those gallows," ordered the king. And it was done.

Queen Esther then told the king
that she and Mordecai were cousins.
And Queen Esther begged the king
to stop Haman's evil order to kill the Jews.

King Ahasuerus had Mordecai write another order, and it was signed with the king's name.
This order said that the Jews could defend themselves against the people who came to destroy them.
And the Jews were victorious over their enemies and were saved from death.

Ever afterwards, a great feast day has been held
on the day the Jews were saved.
It is called Purim, after the lots Haman had thrown.
On Purim, Jews give gifts to the poor and one another.
This spring holiday often falls during Lent,
when Catholics recall the courageous faith of Queen Esther.

Printed in July 2021 by DZS, in Ljubljana, Slovenia
Job number MGN21038-02
Printed in compliance with the Consumer Protection Safety Act, 2008